GHOST, LIKE A PLACE

10 9 8 7 6 5 4 3 2 1

Alice James Books are published by Alice James Poetry Cooperative, Inc., an affiliate of the University of Maine at Farmington.

Alice James Books
114 Prescott Street
Farmington, ME 04938
www.alicejamesbooks.org

Library of Congress Cataloging-in-Publication Data

Names: Pollock, Iain Haley, author.
Title: Ghost, like a place / Iain Haley Pollock.
Description: Farmington, ME : Alice James Books, [2018] | Includes
    bibliographical references.
Identifiers: LCCN 2018020581 (print) | LCCN 2018022181 (ebook) | ISBN
    9781948579513 (eBook) | ISBN 9781938584954 (paperback)
Classification: LCC PS3616.O5696 (ebook) | LCC PS3616.O5696 G56 2018
(print)
    | DDC 811/.6--dc23
LC record available at https://lccn.loc.gov/2018020581

Alice James Books gratefully acknowledges support from individual donors, private foundations, the University of Maine at Farmington, the National Endowment for the Arts, and the Amazon Literary Partnership.

Cover artwork by: Seth Clark, sethsclark.com

GHOST, LIKE A PLACE

POEMS

IAIN HALEY POLLOCK

ALICE JAMES BOOKS
FARMINGTON, MAINE
ALICEJAMESBOOKS.ORG

CONTENTS

III. SOUND

IV. GHOST

V. PLACE

VI. SOUND

VII. GHOST / PLACE / SOUND

FOR NAOMI, ASA, AND ISAAC

Even a ghost is like a place
your glance bumps into with a sound
                    —Rilke, "Black Cat"

An Abridged History of American Violence

The boys are kicking over garbage cans
and smashing car windows with heaves
of glass bottles. Time in the pest house
of school or remediation on a road crew

has moved them to boredom with bare knuckles
and stolen knives. Soon, their insecurity
will concentrate on the grip of a Glock

till an enemy, who a minute before
was unknown and not an enemy, appears
under a streetlight. The provocation
will be slight: soft palms hardened

to a shove. In days to come,
friends of the enemy will strip bark
from the few trees they know and graffiti

their grief onto the trunks. And the boys,
even after the votive jars have filled
with rainwater and plastic rose bouquets
have somehow wilted in the humidity,

the boys will also mourn their killed.
In their woe they will want for a light
to slow-drag through them, a light

like the reflection of sequin or chrome.
They will not find it and they will not
find it until they are discovered faceup
in a dirt lot where neighbors remember

a house, a while back, was torn down,
where now bricks and teeth of glass
push up, like Indian bones, through the soil.

GHOST

We, the Rubber Men

We gunned each other down,
gunned each other down in the street, abandoned

each other unburied. Later, those left bearing
the palls burned to show their love. Burned to light

our streets with the dying asterisms of their rage.
And we watched until our watching made of them

a carnival: He, the twirling fire-spitter.
He, the glass-walker. He, the sword-swallower. He,

the smiling bullet-catcher. From our vantage,
we allowed ourselves to admit no wrong. No

wrong. We were only watching. We were only
breathing in. Breathing in. Breathing in the ether

of routine and accumulation. When we came to,
the field, where in fall children trotted back and forth

like a cloven herd, eddied with snow. Wind-driven snow,
the field buffeted with thin, cold clouds along its camber.

Wind-driven, an uprising of whirls gathering
into the clawed shape of a loss we did not know

we felt. That we would have said was not ours.
That returned into itself. That returned into itself,

no trace. Like breath into breath. Snow into snow. Flesh
into flesh. That leaving no trace, could not be ours.

Violets for Your Furs

Garbage men in this city
don't see fit to put the garbage
in the garbage truck, and in the streets
the dented bottles and cans spin

and roll like the gait of a man
clutching a brown-sacked beer
in his hand. The discount grocer
on Girard sells week-old cuts of pork

and tins of black beans a day
from expiry. And the antique dealer
by the bus stop hawks one-eyed
dolls and green vases. I haven't once,

in eight years, seen the store open
for business. In *Dancing Girl with Castanets*,
the model for the figure's head, Gabrielle
Renard, is posed with rouge on her cheeks,

a garland of indulgent red peonies
in her hair. She looks bored.
And I know this boredom
from Rhea Humphries' eyes in school

when I told her, again, *I love you*.
As for the girl's body, for his gaze
Renoir never paid Georgette Pigeot,
arms bared in a diaphanous *traje*

de flamenca more Hellenic than Iberian.
I can guess now why Rhea never protested
in the halls when I'd stare so brazenly
at her tits. Will I always want something

other than what I have? Which is to wonder:
who knows if I ever loved Rhea? Probably not,
as maybe the young can never love,
or not the young as blindered as I was.

Let's just agree, Gabrielle, let's just agree,
Georgette, I went about it all wrong.

The garbage men are back, girls:
Bottles and cans, cries the heart,
bottles and cans. Bottles and cans,
cries the heart, *bottles and cans.*

Never Drink a Six-Pack in Sight of Jesus
(If You Want to Keep Your Faith)

Summer nights after summer jobs: The Grotto.
Which wasn't one. A clearing in a copse
at the edge of St. Margaret's House. But dank
with condensation under those boughs
as we thought a grotto must be. Talk. Beer.
Teasing. Beer. Beer. Groping & tongue
in the bushes, if you were blessed enough.
Or she enough unbound. Talk. Beer. Above all,
our own rules. Behind a screen of hemlock
& too far down a dirt track to be seen
from Jordan Road. Too far from the convent
to be heard. And those sisters, Episcopalians
& almost obsolete, turned in early. Talk. Beer.
Teasing. Trickle of creek in near-to-dry bed. Rush
of rare passing car. At the clearing center, stood
a plaque & monument: The Wayside Cross.
Removed from the way. And not a cross,
bronzed Christ nailed into the pinewood.
Beer. Beer. Groping & tongue. Our own rules.
And only deaf & blind Him to arbitrate.
When we arrived in last light, though arms
crooked & shoulders sagged to bear His weight,
He seemed serene. Metal not radiant, worn to patina
& dolorous luster. Eyes closed. Hips turned
at a gentle angle. As one bends to find comfort
in sleep. We ignored Him. Beatific Him. Forgot
He was there. Talk. Beer. Beer. Groping & tongue.
Beer. Until a flashlight—every few weeks—caught
His nightly face. The forked beard. The braided
crown barbed with thorns. Eyes alive now, it seemed,
with wrack. Silence. Shadow sway of limb & leaf

over His Suffering. Silence & sway. Silence &
sway. Suffering.

       We left afraid. Through hemlocks
& onto Jordan Road, we left afraid
& swearing we'd never go back.

.

Dates & Inscriptions

Mountains   behind strawberry fields & Salinas
          The Gabilan Range   rise in a color
Californians call   golden   but seems sere
          & lifeless in the midsummer shimmer
We eat lunch in a bank   converted to a pub
          It brews its own beer   drums of malt & yeast

          fermenting   in the old vault   After our meal
we walk out   onto a Main Street lined with blank
          awnings & vacant windows   displaying dust
                    & fog   We pulled into the cemetery
& the way to Steinbeck's grave seemed so clearly marked
          but we're wandering now   scanning stones
for *Hamilton*   Steinbeck buried in his maternal plot

          The child   small in Naomi's womb   (the size
of an orange   growing in a grove along the highway
     between Monterey & here)   slows her pace   drags her
          into fatigue   I'm pushing a search
as she has asked me not to   past what's comfortable
     or healthy   I know I should be   more careful with her
(we have friends   who 20 weeks in   lost their baby)
          but I cannot   I've stepped this far

          When finally we arrive   at Steinbeck's grave
we find the offerings   other visitors have left   quarters & dimes
          brittle copies of his paperbacks   ballpoint pens
open ponderosa cones   a shark's tooth   I look up
     and Naomi has turned back   for the main path
          but stopped   in a cluster of tilted graves
                         we'd passed on our way

     I catch up to her   and see the markers   I'd overlooked
in my hunt   a huddle of infants' graves   their dates & inscriptions

faint   The better part of a week some girls & boys
   survived   but most lived a day   a few hours   no
second sunrise   no name beyond the family   were born
                                & died

Grasping at Swallow's Tail

None of the men practicing
Tai Chai in a field by the river
are Chinese. An impulse tells me
to leave the path that dusts
my shoes with cinders and join them,

but once I tried these movements
and found harmony only
in their names: *Hands like Clouds.*
White Crane Spreads Wings. Search
for Needle on Sea Bottom.

Behind the men, a leaf drifts
along the current. I tell myself
it fell from a box elder—
I've hiked past stands of those trees
beside the creek that feeds this river.

And from these green waters,
the leaf will spill into a broader
brown river, and at the wide bay
where that would empty into the sea,
migrating red knots wing down

each May from Tierra del Fuego,
wing down withered, chests
sunken to breastbones, wing down
to crack open the husks
of horseshoe crabs and gorge,

bulk up to finish the flight
to the tundra, to nests scraped
into the frost-hard earth.
Throw the Loom. Flash Arms
like Fans. And fishermen bait

their lines with crab, and the colony
dwindles, and the shorebirds
die off. And the Black boys
of Philadelphia, this summer,
one gunned down each day.

the smoke of the country went up

Drop fire from the sky but don't name me
as reason. My sister is lost on the longest lit road

in the world. She wanders into shoe stores
the hour before close and chews the stock

back to rawhide. My father's workshop tools
have broken into open rebellion—he worked

and worked them to the bone. Any second now
the circular saw will churn through the basement door

and into the kitchen, gnawing the floor to spit
and sawdust. Out West my cousin has soldered

the mirrored lenses of police-issue sunglasses
over his ocular cavities. All he sees is wrong.

Alert the Department of the Interior: our enemies
are inside the fence. Drop fire from the sky

but don't expect it to purify their hate.
Or, if it does, it'll burn me clean with the rest.

Here's my hope for salvation: when the stranger
comes knocking, open my arms wide with the door

and give him whatever he takes.

whatever wilderness contained there

A woman, her white curls rolled tight, has twice limped through our train car and cannot find a seat. We have passed the zoo and are cutting through North Philadelphia. She complains to the conductor. She is loud, and we are in the Quiet Car. The conductor asks for her ticket and inspects it. Her ticket is for this train. Not our original train, broken down in the station. *If you have a ticket for the Keystone*, he says, *stand up and make room for Vermonter passengers.* He says we were told this before we boarded. We were not.

Naomi and I could not sit next to each other—she is four rows in front of me and across the aisle. She has unpacked her lunch. The conductor is standing over her and sees her ticket. He tells Naomi to stand. I stand and say, *I'll give her my seat.* I do not act out of kindness for the limping woman. *That doesn't matter*, he says. *All Keystone passengers must give up their seats.* He is standing over Naomi. She is gathering her lunch and slow to rise. He insists she leave the seat. We are in the Quiet Car. The conductor tugs at her elbow, and she drops her sandwich. I step toward him and explain that she is pregnant.

That doesn't matter, he says. *She has the wrong ticket. You were told before you boarded.* I say, *No. We weren't.* Other passengers from the broken-down train mumble in agreement. My voice is rising when I say again, She is pregnant. I do not tell him: early on. First week of the second trimester. Probably, she could make the trip to New York on her feet. *She is pregnant*, I say. Am I acting to protect her? She is carrying a child. *She is not standing*, I say. We are in the Quiet Car. Everyone is staring at me. My jaw clenches.

The conductor is a small man. I am not a small man. Naomi is not standing. She is pregnant. I am standing. Close to the conductor. Over the conductor. My jaw clenches. *I'll throw you off at Trenton*, he says. *Fine with me*, I say, *but she is pregnant. She is not standing.* He says, *I'm throwing you off at Trenton. Great*, I say, *but if I'm getting thrown off, you're getting thrown off, and everybody else is getting thrown off. Except her*, I say, *because she's pregnant, and she's not standing.* This is not rational. Am I acting to protect her? We are in the Quiet Car. My jaw clenches. Naomi is looking up at me. I have seen this look before when I have yelled—like a skittish dog. Am I acting to protect her? She is pregnant. She is carrying a child.

The conductor is a small man. He is no longer threatening me with Trenton. He is making a semantic argument: *You can say she's pregnant*, he says, *but you can't say that she's not standing*. I laugh. I am winning. *No*, I say, *I'm saying she's pregnant and she's not standing*. We are in the Quiet Car. People are staring at me. I'm staring at the conductor. The breath moves fast through the knot in his throat. My jaw clenches. He is a small man. I am winning. He shakes his head. He turns and sidles down the aisle. I have won. When he comes back, he will not look at me. I have won. Naomi is sitting. We are in the Quiet Car. She is pregnant. Early on. Was I acting to protect her? She is carrying a child. I have won.

PLACE

Brewerytown

This morning, the lovers—
who last night were slurring and stumbling
and when I looked out, each gripping
the other's taut throat in a clench of callous
and nail, each forcing gritted teeth inches
from the other's face—sit on their front steps.
The woman smokes an idle cigarette. The man lounges
two steps down from her and leans his head
into her lap. Beer cans and husks of blue crab
from their cookout scuttle by in the languid breeze.
The woman flicks the stub of her cigarette
into the street and kisses her man on the forehead.
A whir and scrape, in the kitchen behind me,
a whir, whir, and scrape, burrs grating
in the coffee grinder that Naomi jolts on.
I frown back at her but don't bother to complain
about the racket this time. I'm more interested in
the lovers. Or, I was—they're tender now and tedious.
I liked them better when the radio was pumping
from their open window, and they were clawing out,
under the streetlight, the terms of their love.

The Road Will Be My Last Idea

The park is stripped down for winter,
and I won't be here when it transforms
to a green cathedral, all still and solemn

in the high humidity—we leave the city
in June. This commute, these acres of gray
trunks sprawling up slopes on either side

of the road, will be my last idea of this town.
With all the bareness, even at speed, I can see
far into the woods, the only hint of foliage

deep green ellipticals of rhododendron curling
in the cold and the blanched, marcescent leaves
that beeches refuse to drop. A stone wall

lines the road margin where a creek ran
until the city tunneled its water into a sewer line.
(A gap for a footbridge still interrupts the masonry.)

Before the park, the houses were like the one
I just left, where my wife is shading her eyes
and straightening her cardigan. Now that the road

has wound out of the valley, the houses have changed
from brick and flat-roofed to gabled and stone—
same rock as the wall, schist hauled up from the bed

of a broader creek this road followed before bending
toward the buried tributary. On a stretch of pavement
here, every morning, I see the same woman

walking her beagle as it strains against its lead, the same
man dashing toward Upsal and the train. Above us,
the sun burns a light spot in the ashen expanse

of cloud, a dull shine like an answer to a question
about a time or place that I know I should know
but cannot, cannot bring myself to remember.

Baldheaded Woman's Burlesque

Adult chatter about the swallows' return
to the mission at Capistrano bored me,

and I snuck off to explore the house. The best secrets
were always in bathrooms: an unopened box

of condoms, an old nude photo of the hosts
soaking in a tub, and in the long vanity cabinet,

the wife's wig stands, chestnut bobs resting
on four, a fifth empty. I laughed of course,

when I imagined her naked scalp, never
pausing to ask why the hair had fallen away.

That was the devil of a kid's mind: I mocked
what I could not know, laughed at wigs,

at the shame I felt over a baldheaded woman,
laughed at both the body's devouring long division

and its thinning hope of resolution—that burlesque
of pride she pulled tight over her bare crown

while she sacrificed herself to live.

Prayer to Be a Vessel of Mercy
Expressed as a Newtonian Equation

It must have been blind,
and it was dying.
Some rodent, its fur pulled
taut on its bones,
scraped across the sere grass,
out in the open.
              The first of us
snatched a rock, took aim,
and hurled it.
              The rest followed,

stopped our hillside war
waged by neon water pistols,
by green balloons stamped
with the geometry
of grenades.
            A slow barrage
began, one chuck at a time,
the entire group tracing
                   the arc
of each stone.

With lob after lob,
we did not hit
that dying mass. Stray throws
provoked from the group
crows and hoots
at piss-poor technique,
at weakness of arm
or vision.
          We were right
to think ourselves flawed:

a retreating animal,
hunching lower and zagging
with each rock that landed
grass blades from its sick skull,
stalked by a troop of boys
that every near miss—
concussive thud in the hard,
dry earth—
           brought to a thrill.

Soon the dying thing
crawled too far from us,
               out of range,
and the arcs and impacts
lost our interest.
             We found new games,
sent rocks through the high crook
of a eucalyptus, raced up
and down the hill, triggered blasts
of water at friends imagined
as enemies.
          Then, one by one,
we were called
        to dinner.
              We dragged
along the slope,
        grumbled
about the summons

into houses,
      out of the world.

But while we filled our guts,
the rodent,
       off in the grass
or in the hill brush,
must have died, the cause
a force not propelled
by our hands.
       In that hour

or the next, the thing ceased, killed
not by us—mercy
                    of angle
and motion, mercy of distance
and time, small mercy,
                        great mercy—
killed not by us,
            not by us.

Constellations of Our Own Making

The three of us would sit on the floating
dock, the wake of night boats
slapping on barrels and sodden wood,
and shout to girls somewhere

in the darkness across the lake.
What we'd say to them in the night,
we'd never have said to their eyes.
When no girls were in earshot,

the Holmes brothers and I would look
skyward for the Dog Star or gamble
on who could count the most satellites
or trace fingers between points of light

and give lewd name to constellations
of our own making. One night a canoe
full of girls pulled within twenty yards
of the dock: sweet, high voices

called to us, beckoned us to swim out
from our berth and to them. We stood
mute a moment, looked back and forth
between us, then fled, howling

and barefoot, over exposed tree roots,
up the trail to the A-frame camp house.
Within the hour, we were asleep
in our hiding spots. Come sunrise

and the morning water's glassy calm,
we bragged that our slick talk had lured
the canoe across the lake and toward us.
Until called for breakfast, we fit

binoculars over our eyes, scanned
Brantingham's near and far shore
but saw not one moving body—the girls,
if they had ever existed, were gone.

Indian & Colored Burial Ground

We buried Uncle Keith in Nondaga Cemetery,
the old Indian and Colored graveyard where Haleys
have been put in the ground since Carlos bought himself
free of slavery. A crab apple had just come into flower
near Keith's plot. With each breeze, a snow of petals
covered the turned-over soil while we told stories.
I remembered playing basketball in the driveway.
Keith was walleyed and crippled by hard living—
he didn't hit a shot all afternoon. The best story
came from Keith's days working at the VA Hospital.
One night his friends set up a corpse to spook him
when he walked into his shift at the morgue.
Spook he did—back through the door,
his high-yellow face losing its last traces of color—
and didn't come into work till three hours later.
After the service I stayed in a fleabag across Route 15
from a train yard. A chain link fence curling off its posts
separated a mangy lawn from a break of trees. The lights
from Corning shone over the louring, still-bare
branches of those trees, and picnic benches rotted
on the lawn. They had the emptiness of rooms
in a clapboard house where no one will live
after a drifter, a dozen years ago, butchered
a family there. I was glad, in the morning,
when I woke up alive.

III

SOUND

Arrival: Troy, New York

> *And the migrants kept coming.*
> — Jacob Lawrence, The Migration Series (Panel 60)

(Them firebombed.

        (This street: not ours,
           then no one's)

Them shovel-handed
new help.

        (Scabs scabbed over)

Them erstwhile writers
of glyphs in the dust.

      (We backtracked the plow furrow
          to the foundry,
      the mule trace to the beasts'
        tannery-fresh burden.)

We went.

        (Three-to-a-bed
         never scared us)

Stacked like spoons.
Weighed like sacks.

     (Ungreased arm of the grain scale)

We went.
And the bolts that fastened us each
to each turned bullets, conical
and gleaming,
fell upon us as sun on the storm-ripped
and withering trees of peach orchards.
Further gnarling of the already.

Them night leavers.

     (Blackbirds, like arrows, in the black
               sky)

Them room emptiers.

       (Splinter-rough boards
     never looked sadder or prettier)

Them half-naked station waiters.
Them mountain tellers.

                                        (Though
                              we be game-legged)

Them rain-swollen-river crossers.

                                        (*Rock my soul*
                                        in the bosom
                                        of Abraham)

Them blind blind.
Them following-
the-blind blind.
Them blind-
who-ain't-seen.
Them ain't-seen.
Them seen, ain't-seen.
Them.

                                        (Those Them)

Them Them. We Them.
We that Them.
We that traveling Them.
That arrived-and-still-traveling Them.

                                        (That Them)
                                        (Them Them)

That traveling, traveling

                                        Them.)

Cambridge Street Midden

When future archaeologists
excavate the bottom of the embankment
where most of the dead-end block
has thrown garbage, how will they interpret
the heap? The mattress? The corroded tricycle?
The years and years of evergreens?
The terra-cotta sherds?
                              Intact, those flakes
and slivers were two pots that held marigolds
we planted to ward mosquitoes off the front step.
The flowers blanched, and I said I'd move the pots
inside for winter. But that December was so mild
I never did it.
                    January was not so temperate:
snowmelt pooled around the wilted stalks
and froze to a skin of ice covering each pot.
Then, the movement of ice to water, water to ice
and back again did its daily work. The terra-cotta
cracked.
            We fought about it. I had not acted
as I had promised. Floors were stomped. Doors
were slammed. Walls were pounded. Things
were said. Things distantly related to ruined
plant pots. That spring, I scooped the spilled soil
with the pot's own shatters and dropped the mass
down the embankment where it smashed against
the trash of other years, our neighbor's fragments
and our own.
                    When those sherds are exposed
by mattock and trowel, cleaned by probe and brush,
and brought to the sterile lab, what will scholars
studying the urban culture of our time and place see?
An act of beauty, a small gesture against ugliness
and excess? Or a vanity, an immoderation
while those around us lived hand to mouth?
Or a concealment, a burial of brokenness

that our jagged edges might no more confront us
with their stone-aged sharpness?

Liver of Sulfur

Our son isn't due to arrive
for two weeks, but already he knows
the threat and wreck
of this place: a truck slammed

into Naomi's small, blue car,
crumpled its trunk into the back seat,
spilled the rear windshield
onto the Schuylkill Expressway

(the *Sure Kill* said the nodding neighbor
as I rushed to a cab
and the University hospital).

In the perinatal center,
the doctors seemed confident
that Naomi and the boy—
we plan to name him Asa—
were unhurt and healthy.
But their art, all slow drip
and ultrasound, their confidence
is alchemy to me: Liver of Sulfur,
Horn Silver, Fulminating Gold.
How can they know? How do
their beeps and blips rule out
a spinal tear, a contusion
on the brain, uterine rupture?

I can't think about it.

I can't think about it, and for now
I'm sweating in the abandoned,
overgrown lot that verges
on our postage-stamp garden,
and lopping at grasping vines
of wild grape that are bullying

the rosebay we've planted.
I've been reading Borges
and while I hack, I repeat
to myself: *the knife, so intimate,*

opening my throat.
Borges lived, I was surprised to learn,
into years I remember, early grade school,
Turtle Rock Elementary. His name
translates to *of the town. Bourgeois*
if you're cynical. Asa means healer
in one language, hawk in another.

I'm down to the last of the vines,
but before summer ends
I'll have to cut them back again.
the knife,

so intimate. Healer
and hawk. Healer and hawk.
Think of all the people, Asa,
who have lived, as Borges,
while I've lived, all those
who will live while you live.
Those, all those, who will die.

Hysterikos

Kassandra's mistake was the ecstasy
of her protests, her voice like the hiss
of alarm fires, like the clamor of bronze
on bronze. As years ago I accepted

Paris dead in his swaddling on Ida's slopes,
I trusted that homesickness, after a decade,
overcame the Greeks, their sense of duty,
sent the thousand ships back into the Aegean

to their archipelago of hearth and safe harbor.
I was not alone in this certainty. My wife,
behind the palace gates, pining for the lost years,
waited with hook-handled knife and goat sacrifice

for my homecoming. Had Kassandra come to me
with moist eyes over a loom's cracked frame,
a jug shattered on the rocks while returning
from the well, bread left too long in the embers,

I would have drawn her to my chest, smoothed
her hair, and listened. But she foretold my life
in feral prophecies that splattered as afterbirth
falling from a womb. We believe of the future

what we want to believe, no matter the omens
or auguries. I dismissed her and carried on, cocksure.
What little comfort her sooth gives now: the fire spits
and roars inside the city, and bronze does not clang—

deadens against clavicle and shank. With an arm
turned to grit and blood, I claw, reach out past
my wife's dropped knife to a horsehead of shadow,
and know, finally, the rapture and wildness of belief.

Miraculum Vitae

Life is not the miracle. All the dumb mammals
do what we do. Spring after spring, pelts slip

and writhe out of pelts. The miracle is that knowing
what we know, that repeating the lines—again and again

and again—of the only lullaby we can scare to mind,
that bearing cries sharp as their someday canines,

bearing cries that bite into our temporal lobes,
that staggering insomniac with night after night

of shattered sleep, the miracle is we do not find a rock
that fits the shape of our two hands, a sharp hammer

of basalt, and bring it down into their inchoate
softness, the miracle is we empty throats and palms

and let them go on with their mewling, animal lives.

Our Lady of Consolation

I was in a crowded field
and looking for my father.
I caught enough of a beard
and reached for a hand
I thought part of his body.

I did not see the cigarette,
dangling and lit,

until it burned my palm.
At my cry, the hand jerked back
while above it thundered words.

This was not my father.
I could not see him anywhere.

I ran across the field
to my mother, my mother
who enfolded me in her forearms.

She did not let go.

Neither did I, safe then
from all but my need
for body and embrace.

California Penal Code 484

The Irvine cops picked up Sherod
while he was riding Jimmy's bike
to school. He'd snuck up into the scrub hills
above our complex to work on the fort
we were building with wood from a deserted
rancher's shack. By the time he came down
to the bus stop, we were the diesel exhaust
that ferried us to our daydreaming hours.

Jimmy's bike stood in the communal racks.
We all knew the combination to its lock
and took the Huffy as needed. Sherod's need—
to be at Rancho Middle before his father
found out he'd never made it—his need
was one too many. Jimmy's father,
out the door to work, saw his son's bike
gone again, reported it stolen to the cops.
A morning patrol found the bike
underneath a black boy not in school
and hauling ass down Culver Drive.

I did not understand what adult machinations
led to my parents driving that afternoon, with me,
to the Irvine police station. My father
had emigrated from England in the 70s
and was hipped to the American scene as soon
as he started dating my mother. He got out
of our Chevette, looked back at his black wife,
his too-brown son, and said, *Stay put, you two.*

If he pulled that white savior bullshit now,
we'd have words. But I didn't have that term
white savior then. Even if I'd known it,
I don't think I would have used it that day.
Would have cared to use it. My friend was in jail
and headed to juvie, that scare story—whaled on

by high school monsters twice our size—tormenting
our nights and keeping our days straight and narrow.
I didn't care what my father said inside the station,
with what English boys' school curtness he said it,
with what iron-backed code of whiteness. Didn't care
and was happy when he strode out with Sherod

trailing behind him. Sherod, who did not speak
on the ride back to our apartments, who watched rows
of eucalyptus blur by on University Avenue, who
the next morning we avoided at the bus stop,
who did not try to join us, who stood with his back
toward the bike racks, toward Jimmy's bike, fastened
there again, with new lock, with double loop of new chain.

dem kill my mama

Fela Kuti, after soldiers raided his compound
and threw his mother from an upper window, carried
her coffin to the barrack gates for the reason

Mamie Till opened her son's casket and let the world
see Emmett's head like a caved-in gourd,
his neck burned for bearing the gin fan's mass.

I wish I had some comfort for you. But whatever
kindnesses we've suffered—the strange men rocking
our cars out of the snowbank, the silent neighbor

picking up our spilled groceries—here and now
the sunlight passing through the last days
of catalpa leaves and onto the steering wheel cannot

bring the shy stutter back to our children's tongues,
cannot sit our mothers, feet crossed at their ankles,
back in their good, burgundy-upholstered chairs.

I can offer no relief. And no return. All I have for you
is your own body, larynx still sore with the wailing,
shoulders stooped from balancing splintered wood,
from carrying on their creased plane that final weight.

when mud daubers nest

on the underside of the sill,
                         when light
reflecting on snow pinks the sky,
                              when
staghorn sumac sprout between blocks of schist

in a ruined millrace, when yesterday's rain
freezes in a pothole,
                         and morning glories
twine on chain link fences and a trowel blade

cleaves in three a wintering ring snake,
                                   when
the waist-length field grass browns
and breaks flat,
                    when the perpendicular old woman
shuffles in her housecoat on sleet-slick cement,
when steady rains rust tinplate cornices,
                              when sparrows
shake their wings in the dust,
                              when the Pleiades show,
when pot-bound azaleas burgeon
no flowers and deer blood smears the road

and the burden of ice brings down a limb,
when katydid calls slow,
                    I will be standing
between porch posts,
                    tracing the glacial,
night-dark ridges across the valley,
                              or I will not be,
when katydid calls slow,
                         katydid calls slow,
katydid calls slow,
                    when katydid calls slow

GHOST

An Old Country

I don't remember his name. I do remember that the other boys didn't like him. They said he smelled like burned cabbage and ate grass by the handful. After a soccer game, his mother took us to a flea market. We horsed around at one of the stalls and tossed a hand mirror back and forth. I couldn't catch one of his throws and dropped the mirror. The face and plastic case shattered. When the woman who ran the stall yelled, spittle flew from the corners of her mouth. Still, she refused to take money for the mirror even when the boy's mother offered to pay. We met once, after the soccer season ended, to kick the ball around. A stray dog came to the field and ran loud, frothing circles around us. I remember that I was afraid. When the dog scampered off, the boy's grandfather, who had been watching us play from a small rise, walked down and handed us long sticks. He was from an old country. I don't remember which one. Iran? He said something to my friend. It was not in English; I did not understand. My friend brandished the stick: He says *next time the dog comes, we should hit him hard in the head until he stops barking.* The dog didn't come back. I remember being happy it stayed away. A few years later my family moved from California to New York. Today, this is all I know about him.

On the Migration of Black Oystermen from Snow Hill, Maryland to Sandy Ground, Staten Island

What flag will fly for me / When I die?
—Langston Hughes

From a distance, my flag
and star could be you. I could be.
If I weren't, my body—the place
would still have need of it. No
Romanesque without me. I am.
I am. And the price of my being:
no monuments built me. None
save those cradled in crabgrass,
left for chicory. No monuments
but the air breathed. The history
of arches and burning
hearts. The history of false teeth
and matches. No monument
but the knowledge gained in overrun
gardens: yellow-ringed snakes
and plumage of undiscovered
birds. But the topography
of mountains we have yet
to scale (looming forever
in the haze).
      My body, your body—
all our lives we have known
each other. Your arms clung
to porch columns. Mine painted
the fence in whitewash. Mine stood by
the gate and held it, every morning, open.
You saw me once. You do not see me.
My talk to you comes out a backward
cacophony, the chattering of crows
in the field's distant sycamore.

You do not see me. You do not
see me. No monument
you'd ever recognize. A flutter.
A spring hinge. A flush
of violet above tough stalk.
A line of char in the soil.
A catch, in your lungs,
of cold air. I am. I could be.

A Lament, from Greener Territories, for the Row House

The iron post, wrought
into a hook and painted black:

at the new house, wood on stone foundation,
I staked its sharp end between boxwoods
and hung a cage feeder for the birds.
When the raucous jay, mimicking in call

a red-tailed hawk, landed on the hook's dark
curve, he shocked away a quarrel of sparrows.
He hopped to the feeder and pecked at seed
before flitting back to the hook, turning twice,

jeering, and then flapping into the sweet gum.
With the jay's departure the post shook and shook
(spilling birdseed into the grass) and stayed shaking
when the sparrows (field, song, house) flew back

to chirp and feed. Down the sloping lawn,
a single apple tree, branches beginning to sag
with ripening, did not shake in the humidity.
I am telling this to you, but it will not translate

to the grit and brick of your syllables. You are there.
I am here: summer, boxwoods,
birdsong, swelling,
                swelling,
                        swelling.

The Changing Table

While the doctor sutured Naomi
and the nurses cleaned her blood
from the delivery room floor, I held my son,

his shape and small heft calibrated
for my arms, and I was sure. I was sure
and then the months-long refusal to sleep.

How could these midnight caterwauls
be of me? How could I love a thing
devouring my time, a thing goading me

into insomnia? But this afternoon
lying supine on the changing table,
the boy achieves an improbable feat:

he sends an arc of artesian-clear piss
onto his own face. He's shocked at first—
the slight sting of diluted urea in the eye—

but breaks into a grin when I can't stifle a laugh.
Then another laugh and another slip out
until I'm bent in half and trembling, head low

as I try to hide my delight at the indignity
I've seen his face suffer. Hide it I can't, and
between my laughing and the trickles of urine

down his milk-fat cheeks, his soft gut spills
into its own laughter. I wipe his face then
and pick him up. His calves tumble over

my right arm, his fit in my embrace
not as snug now as that first hour,
but his laughter shakes inside my chest

and rolls through me like the certain ring
of a swing set's galvanized post drummed
and drummed with the thick end of a stick.

Hurricane Season

The past-peak goldenrod lashes in a second day
of raw-throated wind that in the night swept
white hickories off their limbs and into the lawn

where—small meat hulled behind bone-thick
husks—they rot into ground. This rain and gust,
the front edge of a late-season hurricane, its eye

churning now over the water-worn limestone
of Bahamian islands, before its forecast turn north,
up the American coast. We have not spoken

this week. Not since Sunday when for reasons
I could not—cannot—explain, I slammed the door
to the bedroom off its top hinge. Coming north,

the storm will likely veer east, out into the Atlantic,
leagues off Cape Cod. But if it hooks west,
makes landfall at a near shore, we'll have to talk

about the tree closest the house, the diamond-ridged
white hickory, whether it can withstand the howling,
can hold upward its wind-shaken branches,

save them from downward flight, from ripping
through shingle and rafter, save them from cracking
through the crosswise joists that brace our gabled roof.

topography (inland)

if asked then,
i would have said *lost*:
the pacific breaking
into fog (cold saline
air: me a shroud
in a shroud)—
        now & inland,
     here's the hard fact of it: piled,
a demarcation, undulating with up-slope
& down-slant of fields gone to spurge & buckthorn:

this wall's dry stone
        never breaks,
never fogs,
     can never be tidal
   & the sea

Love, oh love, oh careless love

Fucking can't stand when I
slice a grapefruit to an uneven
split. For this small fault, I'm cursing
myself even while I replay the scene:
my student comes red-rimmed
to me and starts to spill—
her work unfinished, her essay
(Bradbury's images of innocence
and corruption) not started. She'd found
a lump. A surgeon would have to cut.
She was scared. She was sorry, her work
unfinished. I did not curse her small fault.
Forgave it. No matter that essay. No curse
for her, only for me—the cockeyed cut
of the grapefruit—while my son,
couchbound in mother's arms, roasts
with his third day of fever. Unable to walk.
Tottering more than usual on new legs.
And after long today, a third night
I will hold him, wailing him,
him destined to small faults—
the broken glass, the crayoned wall—
soothe him with song and hands
until he falls asleep. Until his body
is limp and small, unhearing
of song, unfeeling of hands.
All this—but a grapefruit, ruby,
tropical and paradisiac ruby,
split like I can't fucking stand,
two halves uneven, grossly,
no small fault, cursing myself,
me, me, careless me. No
proportion. No poise. Careless,
careless me: have I taught
the girl better than I've taught
myself? And have I loved

the boy better than I've loved
myself? Which is careless (me)
love. Which is no love at all.

Where Do We Come From? What Are We? Where Are We Going?

These are not the lyrics to the lullaby
playing in my son's room: *Paul Gauguin
ain't no time to be wastin   in the end
we're all junkies*   The boy cannot sleep.
And if he cannot sleep, I cannot sleep
until my delirious hope for his sleep
muddles the song's half-heard language
with my thinking on Gauguin, the capacious
noble-savage canvas in the museum's exhibit.
Sunk on the floor, head resting on the wall
at nerve-pinching angle, I churn

in this eddy: *in the end we're all junkies*. Is this
worth it? Do I sit in an unlit corridor, go in
and out, in and out of my son's room, rock him
for glacial epochs, deprive myself of sleep
to the edge of reason, and he turns out broken
as Gauguin, broken as any of us can be. Childish
in our vision of the world. So embarrassed
by the naïve and the naked we turn frantic
for a fix. Or so ashamed we imagine an escape,
some bogus Arcadia, some nubile paradise
of the tropical and willing, where

we keep hanging on, where we find
some tempting tongue of flame. Where
we find the next fix. And the next fix.
Where we stumble upon some childhood
(bull thistle and deer skull down by the trestle?)
wrapped neatly in guilt and sorrow. The next fix.
And the next.
              Where we keep hanging on.
Our teeth detritus in the dawn-gold pool
of gutter. And the next fix. Miasmas of vomit

and remorse. And the next. Keep hanging on.
The next fix.

        And the next. Hanging on. And
the next fix. And the next. And the
next fix. And the next—

                till we can't

be fixed

       no more.

The Overworld

in shadow she trailed shadow.

when i turned to face her,
she weaved between the mottled,
peeling trunks of sycamores
back the way we had come
then dissolved like last notes
of a radio's static nocturne
into the high cattails
and banked morning fog.

       i had enjoyed the night,
the pursuit, and was sorry
to see her go.

       you and i met
the next summer,
your approach the pop
and flash of filament burning out,
a burst impressing the closed eye
with a promise of daybreak
even as it scatters the flurry
of moths, brings the narrow porch
to dark and cool.

         today, a decade
of summers gone, while you shut off
lamps and drew down blinds, i stood
on our front step. looking back
into the shaded hall, i half expected
you weren't there.

       but out of the dimness,
your shape and strut.

you brushed past me,

led us down the street
where the sun radiated
from tracts of asphalt,

where pine boards nailed
across cavities in the brick
swelled and warped,

where in the oven air
picked-over meat on rib bones
turned seeping and sour.

      you led
and did not disappear,

      remained with me in this:
the too-bright world.

V

PLACE

The Properties of Solid Phase Materials

I. *Early Rain*
All week, ice laid scabrous on the road
and rutted where out of necessity cars
had made their way. We grew to think,
toward the end, this state would last
forever. And then this morning, a warmer rain.
The runoff thawed channels into the ice
and by afternoon washed away the sheet.
Only thick puddles bore testament
to our earlier fears. For a few hours,
we walked steadily, with less concern
for bruising our tailbones. But why did I ever
stop my worrying? Why don't I ever notice
the darkness gather and spread? Now,
the sodium vapor buzzes in the streetlights,
and this rain, as I thought I heard it promise
never to do, has turned again into solidity,
slick and glinting, fixed and hard.

II. *Late Snow*
Last week, you and the boy moved out,
to New York. We'll be back together
by June, but any absence—the dash out
for milk, the walk to the mailbox—carries
the threat of permanence. Will distance
make us bitter as the beginning
of our inclement spring? This morning,
a cold rain corroded patches of exposed
wrought iron where black paint
has flaked off the rail. And the afternoon
turned colder still: by dusk, snow fell,
clotting icy-white on the pink cherries come
into tentative bloom at the street corner. I know
this is the last snow, maybe one more at worst,
and this time tomorrow the coating will be runoff

in a storm drain. I know the cherry blossoms
will have scattered in a month and given way
to a verdure of toothed leaves. And by June,
I know, just as today I thought the snow
would never end, I'll let myself believe our days
of warm and green could go on and on forever.

To Know Its Taste

The oleander grew along a stucco wall.
My mother said the flowers were beautiful,
the leaves deadly. I should not eat them.
But I'd never have thought to take the leaves
onto my tongue without her warning.

Other dangers lurked: coyotes killed the cats
we'd brought out West. Just outside our latticed gate,
I saw one. Her yellow-eyed stare urged me to kneel
in the dry grass. Then, with a blink, she spared me
and loped into the chaparral. I watched her climb

a trail through scrub oak and whitethorn and crest
the first ridge. Not long after, I chewed an oleander leaf.
I wanted to know its taste. My mother forced me
to drink from the milk jug until I vomited,
and I survived. The summer after my poisoning,

she moved me away from California, back East.
In this city, the rain fell all afternoon and threatens
to fall again. Across the narrow street, behind candle jars
painted with Virgin Mothers and armed angels,
a baby boy has been awake all night. A woman tries

to soothe him, but he yowls and yowls at a moon shining
over hills he does not yet know. But one afternoon
when able, he will walk into those hills, and—yellow eyes,
whitethorn, distant waning, serpent hid beneath sweet
flower—he will know them, each ridge, each ungentle slope.

The fig that, as it falls,

                              splits
on cement is not like making love
on the basement couch.
                              The start a sparrow gives
as it flutters too close to the face
is not like the shock
and laceration of shattered glass.
                              The jangle
of the ice-cream truck is not like the sweat of palms
slipping from monkey bars.
                              Turning suddenly
into the aisle, the slender-hipped woman,
flowers in the crook of her right arm,
her basket hanging empty on the left,
is not like the closing screak of a gate
left open in the rain.
                              Neither
is the gooseneck gourd on the stone steps
like the grace of a black-footed gander beating
it wings to land in the morning river,
                                        nor
is the toddler's word for geese—*eese*—
like a gosling trying to cross the parkway
without its gaggle,
                    nor
                              is the tick of ice-rain
on the trolley window like the hiss of steam
circulating into the radiator.
                              When I stepped
onto the slick sidewalk, I nearly broke
my neck. Three more times,
on the walk from Baltimore to Osage,
I almost slipped and shattered my hip,
as did my red-haired aunt one Flushing winter.
I was stranded on a flight from Denver and glad
to arrive at my friend's house. I drank water

in such flow that his wife

                       (she wasn't a mother then,

but maybe she was pregnant)

                          warned I'd grow kidney stones

if I ever slowed my thirst. She was right—

like the biting, crystalline tear of salt

and calcium in the organs—she was right,

and I was wrong:

                    just as writing *I nearly broke / my neck*

is the half-deaf baritone a great uncle bellows

from the back pew,

                   so the limp gosling lying

against the parkway curb—the rushing cars

causing the feathers on its upturned chest

to ripple—

               is the young mouth's missed

sound: *eese*

      eese

      eese

Squall

Across the vine-tangled alley,
a hole cracked open
                              in our neighbor's
          disused chimney.
As I stood by the window
                    watching,
it gaped larger
                    while rain and snow,
the cooling and warming of air,
worked bricks loose
                         from mortar
and sent them, with the force
of their own weight,
                         thudding below
onto the flat roof.
                         I should not
have watched this happen.
                         Not daily
as I did.
          In the next room, my son
was squalling.
               Soon, tongue to teethridge,
he will begin to form the word
                              lonely.
Lonely.
               The air is cold again.
          The sky,
                    behind the chimney,
looms low
                    and gunmetal gray.
Around the hole, bricks
                    come looser
and looser
               in their interrupted rows.
Because I do not know
                    what happens next

I should go to him
                    but I cannot turn
        toward the boy
                    and away,
        cannot turn
toward him and miss the spectacle
        of these certain things:
                gravity,
                        decay.

The Field

He wanted to take a Yamaha he'd bought
back to the farm and asked for help
rolling it into the bed of his pickup.
I was useless. A hindrance, if anything.
In the end he pushed the bike into the truck
by himself. He still took me for beers
at The Field, where on the condom machine
in the men's room someone had scrawled:
for refund insert baby.

                        Joy has its blowback,
I knew that then and know it now.
Headed home from a city night,
like the one we had at The Field
after I couldn't help him
with the Yamaha, he was driving
that same midnight-blue truck
when he hit a patch of black ice
and spun off the road. The fender
smashed to junkyard scrap. His neck
snapped—

            fuck—I'd take it all back,
all the raucous, carousing nights,
the half-remembered fun leading
to good stories punctuated in morning
bruises, I'd take back ever knowing him
to be free of saying

                        His neck

snapped—

            but what happened stays
happened. I knew that then. I know it now.
To wish otherwise is useless, like a father
regretting the day his son was born, like a man
watching his friend push a motorcycle

up a bowing two-by-eight, watching
that friend make the top and breathe
deep, breathe deep, stretch back
aching shoulders and breathe deep.

Blue Jay Restaurant (29th & Girard)

Two cops hover over a group of boys
who have their feet spread and their hands
pushed up against an azure-tiled wall
outside the Blue Jay.

One of the twins is in the lineup,
and when I see him, I stop short
on my way to the trolley. The twins' names
are DaVon and DeVon,

and the older one is bigger, say the neighbors.
But I can't tell them apart, and not when one twin
passes by without the other. I just know
they both go by *Von*,

and I can't go wrong. The drunks congregating
around the scene mumble that the cops
want the boys against the Blue Jay for a rash
of Avenue stickups.

I can't understand that. Whichever Von this is,
maybe he's into bad shit off the street,
but on the street he calls me, *Mister Iain*,
and when he says it,

he looks me in the eye. The other Von too.
The worst they've done in my sight: throw
empty liquor bottles onto the train tracks
below our blind alley.

Nothing I didn't do as a kid. Nothing
I haven't seen grown men do. And I never
saw it happen again. The smaller of the cops
standing over the line

is still a big, bullnecked guy, and when he orders

Von to turn around and face him, he also shoves
a shoulder blade, spinning the boy forward.
I see Von see me,

and say, *Leave him alone—he's a good kid*,
and the other cop, the real big one, stares me down
as if he just witnessed me smash and grab
in broad daylight

and can't wait to slam me into the concrete.
I back up farther into the crowd, which has grown
as people waiting for the always-late 15 trolley
join the drunks.

The smaller cop starts barking at Von and his friends.
I can't hear their responses, can just see them shake
and nod, shake and nod until, with a final push for Von,
the cops let them go. The friends split

in different directions, a pair of them north up 29th,
a pair east on Girard, and Von by himself to the west.
I wheel around the crowd and think to catch him up,
but he's moving fast,

and I can see the trolley car at the 31st Street stop.
I call after him, *Von, you okay?* And he calls back,
Yeah, Mister Iain—I'm okay, but he doesn't turn
to look at me, keeps his head

cocked down and walks toward our street.
When the trolley creaks to the corner,
he's halfway down the block. I climb the stairs,
and drop in my token,

which hits the other coins in the fare box
with a dull clink, metal on metal, like the jangle
of cuffs a boy doesn't register as he goes
from cracking jokes

with friends to rammed against blue tiles
and the wall.

Fountain of the Three Rivers

A young boy, a toddler, rocks on the lip
of the fountain in Logan Circle, his mother
and father on either side. He's making a mess
of an ice-cream cone, strawberry, while laughing
at the twists and stretches of his father's face.

Jamaal's in town, and we're watching the boy
and also the upspray of the fountain as it rises
through the view of the brownstone façade at Basilica
Saints Peter and Paul, its clerestory windows set high,
its vaulted copper dome oxidized to aqua green.

The boy, then, starts laughing too hard and topples
back, down toward the fountain's pool, but his mother
shoots out her arms and braces him. When she pulls
the boy back to sitting, he's laughing, with the thrill
of falling, even harder than before. It's hard not to smile,

this little boy open-mouthed, shaking with laughter,
his brown left cheek covered with a broad daub
of red-pink ice cream. Later, at the museum,
we're standing in the Modern and Contemporary Wing,
staring at a Rothko—one of the color fields, not *Orange*,

Red, *Yellow*, but similar shading on the rectangles—
and Jamaal says *the colors are vibrating*, and I'd never
liked Rothkos until then because, of course,
I'd never understood them. And now I love them.
And now I'll never be able to stop loving them.

VI

SOUND

Tamir Rice

At that enthralling gallop / That only childhood knows.
—Emily Dickinson

Yellow mansion. Lemon Hill.
Lemon Hill. Sun glinting in windows. Same sun
glittering broken glass on court. Balls fly
backwards. From long distances. Through legs.
Balls clang. Clang. Clang. Off iron rim.
Ball caroms to my boy. *Shoot*. He runs
(no dribbling) & releases: five feet up.
Nowhere near rim. Iron rim. But circle of high fives.
For the try. Game begins. Three-on-three.
By ones. Two points beyond the arc. Concussion
of ball. Talk. Clang. Talk. Concussion of ball.
Talk. Clang. Curse. Curse. Ball. Clang. Off
iron rim. Off iron rim & off the court. Across
graffiti sidewalk: *30th Street. Stay out our park.*
Across & into long clover. Lemon Hill. Ball
heaved. Across sun. Onto court. Concussion.
Concussion of ball. Clang. Three-on-two. *Wait up.*
Clang. Off the iron rim & off the court. Again.
Across & into long clover. Again. *Nope—I ain't going.*
Boy lies down. Hands under head. Eyes shut.
To sun. To Lemon Hill. Pleas. Taunts. Taunts.
Pleas. Pebbles. Pebbles. Pebbles. Eyes shut.
My boy next to him, mimic. Lies down. Hands
under head. Eyes shut. A friend caves. Sprints
down slope. Across & into long clover. Lemon
Hill. Ball heaved. Across sun. Concussion of ball.
First boy up. My boy down. Game revives.
My boy still down. On court. Won't stand up.
Won't open eyes. But laughter. Laughter. Up & over
my shoulder. Laughter. Small weight. Closed eyes.
Laughter. Laughter. Tight-eyed laughter. Toward
30th Street & home. Behind us: concussion & clang.

Talk & shout. Curse & curse. Concussion, concussion
& clang. Clang & curse. Concussion. Behind us
& iron rim & six boys & splinters of liquor glass:
mansion windows. Mansion windows. Sun
glinting. Sun. Sun. Sun. Glinting. Glinting.
Lemon Hill. Glinting. Sun. Heavy going-down
sun. Heavy, heavy (glinting) going-down sun.

Aubade

Did you notice me go? You were standing
at the kitchen counter. I did not slam the door.
I pulled it so the lock made the least click

in the latch. Along the road that passes the hospital
where you will bear our second son, that forks
as it runs out of town, I saw a crow perched

on a wire. Flapping its wings, it rose on its talons
but did not fly away. If my windows weren't closed
against the cold of a tailing year, I would have heard

the crow caw when it thrust forward its head
and throat. In the windshields of oncoming cars,
the rising sun glanced sharply. When I do not sleep

tonight, should I dream you a dancer in a coat
of dark, iridescent feathers, or the freshly sliced
pear's dripping juice on a knife blade? And me—

should I dream me a whorl of road, forgotten
entrance and blocked exit, or a pinewood door
slammed on sobs in the other room? I'll ask

again: did you notice me go? I hope not.
These autumn mornings I've tried to shut out
all auguries, all evidence of my own going.

Black Cock

The night before school ended,
in his closet, with a belt,
Bobby Dougherty hanged
himself.

His girlfriend had left him,
and he wouldn't graduate with us—
that's what we chalked it up to.
But grades and a girl
couldn't have been all.
We should have seen
the impulse coming:
how he drank

harder than any of us,
how the tires of his enemies
were slashed with a switchblade,
how he screamed, *You fucking
wetback*, at our school's
only Puerto Rican
before he pummeled
the shit and blood out of him.

We should have seen the sadness
that bursts out as anger,
we should have looked
beyond our own pettiness
and made some human gesture.
And I still can't live up

to that *should have*, can only
think of him that afternoon
he walked next to me
out of the locker room
and, clamping his hand
to my shoulder, asked, *Is it true*

all black guys have big cocks?
I skewed my eyes at him,

expecting his malicious grin or worse
that savage glare, tipping off a flurry
of punches to fatten my lip,
break my cheekbone, my fifth rib.
But his eyes were open—

no spiteful squint—and waiting.
He wanted a real answer.
I didn't have one for him.
All I had for him was me,
quavering as an animal, its foot
caught in tempered steel, willing,
for freedom, to damage itself, to gnaw
through skin and muscle, ligament

and bone. To answer him, I blurted,
Yes, darted past his left shoulder,
and scurried into the hallway,
searching for the camouflage
of other bodies. At a safe distance,
I looked back, and his face
was set again to its malice, unflinching
even when his girl, who wouldn't break it off

for three months more, walked up,
offered her palm, and waited for him
to reach out, to hold on with the cracked-skin
knuckles of his own hand.

Autumn: Far Field, New Moon

I'm leading the seventh-grade boys' soccer team
from the far field to a point, without a marked
crosswalk, where I will shepherd them across the road.

Behind me, together in huddles, they murmur
just softly enough that I cannot hear the particulars
of their gossip (that girlish word they'd never use).

Ahead of us, in a catch of wind, a tulip poplar loses
a tumult of leaves, golden in the reposing light.
This season, we've been practicing on the far field

while the near one is torn up, leveled, laid with artificial
turf. Today, down the length of the field, workmen dig
a drain trench, a thin mound of soil piled along its lip.

Faces salted with sweat, the diggers seem happy
for the end of the day: their chatter cuts quickly back
and forth, and with every few shovel loads, they break

into laughter. Their Spanish is spoken too quickly
and mine learned too long ago for me to make sense
of what is said. When the boys and I reach the road,

a Jeep, painted a dull silver, pulls from the student lot
at the upper school and peels past us toward the church,
St. Martin-in-the-Fields. At the intersection, the Jeep

blows through a stop sign and races over the railroad
bridge beyond it. I walk to the yellow line dividing
the lanes and wave the boys across before more cars

can rip through. I thought myself, at their age, bigger
and readier for the world. In two hours, the sky
will cloud over, and night will fall, moonless and opaque.

Boxwood

The synthesized death rattle of soul music
played on the radio while my father drove us
to the school where he taught and I waited
to be lined up and led outdoors. At day's end,
I was dismissed before he finished with his students.
I'd often gather a group of friends and sneak
to spy on him. Through a grated cellar window,
we watched him in his basement classroom, his hands
white with chalk dust or slapping a wooden pointer
against a map we imagined to chart the position
of enemy guns but depicted a world we'd see redrawn
within a decade. After we exhausted our espionage,
we teetered in the sprawling, low-slung branches
of a yew and crushed clear fluid from its red fruit.
A row of these evergreens—trimmed square
and waist-high—hem the walk into the nursery school
at our synagogue. This afternoon, my day of teaching done,
when I arrive to pick up my son, he'll want to play
on the lawn before I drive him home. He'll find palmfuls
of acorns and throw them into the road to see tires
mash them to pulp. Or, he'll find other boys,
and they'll dash, with the buckling grace of fawns,
under two old boxwoods, pruned to small climbing trees.
They'll clamber there and hang and despite all cautions,
all scolds, they'll fall. And fall. And fall.

GameStop

For Robert Wilson III, Philadelphia Police Department

The boy needs a present (he was
born). And blocks from your boyhood,
you pull in, stop your day to stand
in line, a shirt among other shirts.
It's over quickly: they bluster in
and shout. Smooth motion:
you wheel, thumb flicks, holster
unfastens, palm fits to grip. You
shout. They fire. You fire. They
fire and hit. They fire and hit. You
fall. You fire. You fire. You fire
and hit. No fall. They fire. Gone:
whatever shared hunger and young
dream divided you from them, them
from you, pushed you to this corner
of this room. Gone: whatever son,
whatever imperfect love led you
to this line. They bluster and shout.
They fire. You fire. They fire and hit.
They run. They run. You breathe. You
breathe. Quickly. Hunger. Dream.
Gone. Line. Stand. Line. Gone.
You breathe. Quickly. Hunger.
Gone. Son. Quickly. Stop. Gone.

Magritte's Pipe

By the door to the state-run liquor store,
        the wheelchair-bound man shakes a marimba
           with his change cup. This morning all ideas
have become him. Invalid, negligible, a figment

           of our collective neurosis. *Ceci n'est pas
une pipe*, right? We can trick ourselves & tattoo
such irony on our bodies, but this man is terminus

of all we've been & done since before Genghis Khan
        & long after the atomic bomb. Or let's be honest:

        he is end game of my self-deception, lifetime long
& suckering everyone I know just as their dodges
           & feints beguiled me. Now we're left

with jasmine cascading down the rocks, the redolence
           of linden trees in June not yet turned summer.
        No, not all comes out of Nature—we've pollarded
boulevards of trees to keep them from snarling our wires.

Are these chopped limbs an idea of beauty?
                        This is not:
      if I stand in the right spot, inches
           from where the cat stained the carpet,
I see reflected in my neighbor's window intermittent
        red lights from a skyscraper downtown.
                I watch & in our bed, Naomi,

you sleep. I will lie down for the night & you
        will wake up for a flutter & speak words forgotten
come morning. I will love you more for rehearsing this idea

of our daily failure
              to say anything intelligible
        to one another, signs & signifiers,

                              mirrors,

                                        mirrors,

                              mirrors

without the pretense of smoke.

                         I will love you

as I love the man in his wheelchair.

              His loose change & hard plastic rhythm

        is not,

no matter my need to hear it as such,

                                   a marimba.

And for all my love of him,

              I've been taught never to drop a coin

                         into that cup. I've been taught

no mercy, for others or myself,

              in no quarter, now or ever.

                    Not even if wild riders,

        their horses' hooves beating a pandemonium

                    across the plains, race toward the city limits,

not even if the sky above the towers were to flash

              to deranged blindness & nuclear beauty.

I have been taught,

                    & therefore I have failed. I cannot escape it.

This idea is like a pipe I once saw stuffed & smoldering

                    on the margin of my father's rolltop desk.

        That once I thought could not exist

in the world we know. The world

                              where I will love you more

even if you don't speak to me when we're alone

        in bed, even if you don't stand on sad corners,

even if you don't beg me

                    & beg me for my love.

Not on the sea, not on the sea

Half in the outbound drag of the tide,
half on the wet, glassy sand, his face
turned left and seaward, the boy
lies on his belly, as does my son
in his small bed when, as if a medic
gripping a red gear bag, I hurry

toward him, hoping the mask
of sleep no mask, holding
a forefinger above his lip
to feel on my skin the rise
and fall, the rise and fall
of his breath.

Day 5 (Sunday): *lay thou thy basis sure*

Here's the problem: the day and hour are bright.
Sunlight, outside the window, as it falls through
the remaining leaves of silver maples and pin oaks,
dapples onto the garden grass. The house is quiet

except for the cadenced breathing of the boys
at their afternoon sleep. Can I imagine today
neighbors' names added to a list? Imagine
today the bit in the mouth of the horse arrayed

to drag the carcass outside the city wall? Imagine
the ink of my own name soaking into paper, drying
in the instant of the last pen slash downward?
All I have read and lived has prepared me for this:

I sit with my wife on the couch, our sons between,
our arms like wings draped on the boys' downy shoulders.
From here, we end or we end: the watching and waiting
for the terrible moment—awed by the Leonid shower

of shattering glass, the artful splinter of pressure-treated
pine around the hinge, the pattern of scuff and polish
above a steel toe—or the rising and standing up, the walking
through the threshold to look into the livid capillaries

of an eye, to meet what we must meet, no matter the dark
shine of the hour, no matter the narrow passage of the street.

VII

GHOST/PLACE
/SOUND

Ghost / Place / Sound

(This one's for you, Rex)

(**I.**) Either this happened or that:
$$\text{I was a bastard}$$
or I lied about the circumstance
$$\text{of my birth.}$$

& the date listed on my draft card
differed from what my mama
$$\text{told the Census Man.}$$
thirteen months apart.

$$\text{Five years.}$$
No, I'm not telling this straight:
depending on the folks in front of me,
I was born

        in New Orleans, Memphis, or Chicago.
No, I'm from Duquesne
        or Davenport or Carbondale.
Better yet, Plainfield, Kenner,

Cheraw, Cuthbert . . .
        Or, the lamb-haired uncle,
sermonizing to himself from the corner armchair,
intoned truth:

    We were born unto Saturn.
        Among a race of Angels.

(**II.**) My father taught me to bait hooks
with night crawlers. My mother spoke French & German.
When she died of an enlarged heart, I took shelter

in the churches, writhing & zealous, of my youth.
I became fluent in tongues. But my father, he stayed out,

tasted the drear & cold. In his absences,

I bore strappings whenever my aunties
caught the spirit. Still, I cherished marbles & hobbyhorses
long after friends took to aiming milk bottles at skeletal dogs,

or leaning on lampposts until they shattered.
In the end, however, the neighbors would fear me
above all, hallowed or *haint*.

                    (III.) No, my mama was a charwoman.
On the docks, my daddy unloaded coal. They taught me
that hard work was a degenerative disease. To mourn them,

I became a prodigy: puzzled over primers
& learned to sit still in my seat.
                        No, to mourn them, I dove,

again & again, from the bridge,
                        until the river knocked
the life free from me.

                    No, I mourned them by showboating.
By hiding behind my vernacular. By intimidating,
with my hulk & shout, the other children. I was exiled

& stood in far corners. I watched gangster flicks
& spaghetti Westerns until the hot wind of revenge
angered my high cheekbones.

I began to live
            for the dulcet
                     of girls
                              saying *yes*.

I took liberties with them, begged them to give up
their holy ghosts.
                  When they wouldn't, I snuck off

on riverboats. I stayed out after curfew. I blew

my allowance on firecrackers.
                              I flared up.

          I exploded.
                    I burned down
entire city blocks.

(IV.) In the aftermath,
two fingers, left hand,
little & ring, fused
into one.

            (V.) No, I sewed suits & shined shoes.
I stood on crowded corners with handbills.
I painted signs. Stocked shelves in drugstores
I'd later rob. Laid bricks. Forged steel from the time

I had short hairs. I hawked newspapers
& myself.
          I took degrees in Mathematics
& Chemistry. In Political Science. In Anthropology.

I inspected blueprints. I manned aircraft
never meant to leave the ground.
As conditions demanded,
                    I shuffled my feet.

To avoid contracts & the law,
                    I riffed my name (to Shadow,
to Lockjaw, to Cannonball).
                    I dubbed myself royalty.

I changed my spots
                & told white lies.
I affected Creole, Cuban,
                French, Cherokee & Seminole.

            Anything
          but what I was.

(VI.) I showed up uninvited. Unannounced.
& stayed past my welcome. I danced trots & hops
& shimmies & bottoms. When I drove cross-country,
I towed my Lincoln behind my 'Llac. I wore fur: mink,

fox, coon, didn't matter (long as it was dead).
I stalked San Juan Hill
                            & Bloody Maxwell. I carried a butcher
knife under my coat. Carried bullets

                                   next to my spine.
*   I growled it, smeared it, flatted it,*
sharped it. I brandished pistols in the faces
of my known associates (as none

                           could bear the title *friend*).
I was jammed up for copping Red Devils.
For disorderly conduct (in which case the pigs
beat the *dis* & the *orderly* out of me).

At one point it was Sing Sing
                        or the war.

I took the war
            but kept my head down, stayed
behind the lines & sang the only song my granddaddy
ever taught me:

        For the Land of the Free (cracker)
             and the Home of the Brave (nigger).

(VII.) No, I was a mama's boy. I couldn't hack it
in the city & hightailed it back to the country.

But, forever, I looked down on chitlins & overalls.
For putting on these airs, my enemies taught children

& dimwits to paint masks with my face & sacrifice
chickens to mush-mouthed gods. Which is to say,

those who did not know me made a high priest of me.
A sibyl, a shaman. A bone-in-nose witch doctor.

After my congregation disbanded, I stared at my ceiling
where I'd taped pictures of painted & unattainable brides.

(VIII.) I lost my front teeth
to the cement behind a bar. The taste
in my mouth to a right hook. I took a drunk stumble

onto subway tracks & lost my left arm. You know me now
by the lilt in your stride, the suave on your tongue,
how you always talk yourself out of it,

until one day you don't.

(IX.) (One day TB. Lobar pneumonia. One day terminal
velocity. Of oncoming cars
                              on slick highways.
Of jilted lovers. Of straight razors

in my own hand. One day a doctor's misdiagnosis.
One day the hospital refuses admittance.)

(X.) I tried to break new ground & ended up mired
in the same old swamp. (Which is to say, I failed to live up
to my own expectations.) I lost sleep. I did not mail
the rent check.

        I gave up.
           (One day a scalpel nicks
an artery. One day the balcony cannot bear my weight.)
I pickled myself. I shook with the DT's.

                  My doctor advised me
to stop drinking & I switched from whiskey
to champagne.
        Or committed slow death by cocaine.

I raised a son

in my own image. The public clinic could not save
my daughter. I found excuses—old slight, booked solid,
smacked out—to miss my mother's funeral.

                                        The Blues,
brought on by busted love affairs & brain chemistry,
overtook me. I avoided being seen in public. Wore an overcoat
in Santa Ana summer. In my hotel room,

I set fire to the couch. Then paced, in the lobby, naked.
I checked myself into Bellevue. I turned
into the blue-lit apparition of Creedmoor & Camarillo.
(One day

        uremia. One day cerebral hemorrhage.)

 (XI.) I heard the calling.
                        I found Jesus. Then lost him
among mystics & yogis in the Orient.
I took a vow of silence. (Which is to say,

I learned to bite my tongue.)
                        I came to appreciate the thrum
                        of open space.
Attended the symphony

                just to hear the oboes.
Saw Tokyo & Torino. Paris
                        before the Wars.
The stricken of Calcutta. Tumult in Mexico

& tulips in Amsterdam. Copenhagen, Addis Ababa,
Dear Old Stockholm.

        All the while, I coveted most my neighbor's wife.

(One day I choke on the vomit of my last meal. Go under
anesthesia & never come up.)

                (XII.) I read obscure

German philosophers. I joined the first protest
that happened by. I cast write-in votes
for the soon-to-be assassinated.

I smoked a pipe. Dressed in tweed & corduroy.
Became expert in ceremonial masks of the Fang.
In Hungarian folk music. In a blindfold
test, I could always pick out the Stravinsky.

For my talents, the university gave me tenure
& an honorary degree in survival.
Then, after gum disease slurred my speech,
I retired to the Ozarks to write my memoirs.

I invented every syllable. Especially those about pussy.
But an old flame who knew better found me in my dive,
& we talked till close,
   our voices, smoke-throated,

curled & rasped.
    To the bartender, our longing

sounded better than whatever hysteria
       the kids had racked on the jukebox.

(**XIII.**) No, I shrank like a moldy fig. I hobbled my weight
on a cane & never checked my blood sugar. The IRS
wanted his money. The hospital tab mounted.

But none of this staunched my boast:
in a bar fight, I knocked Joe Louis
to the pine boards. After he stood up—

that I'll never tell.

  (**XIV.**) All in all, I was married ten times
to eight different women. But I spent my last night in the lap
of my love-come-lately, Georgia's deranged indigo heiress.
        (One day

Welfare Island, cirrhosis. Faith healing in Cuernavaca.
Old age, Greenwich. In the British Channel, they
never found the plane. At Columbia Pres., sepsis
& complete shutdown.)

        (**XV.**) My obituary read
like a grandmother's story of me. Like a me
dressed in black & white for Bible school,
scrubbed & shining with Vaseline. (One day cholera

in Jackson. Gut cancer in L.A. One day a coronary
lands me in Woodlawn. In Savannah, black lung.
One day, across the bridge in Englewood,
an ulcer bled me out.)

    (**XVI.**) Either this happened

or that: (One day, skipping the gas
                          & electric, my sister brought
my body to a home
        where I could lay free
                  but could not rest
      my lungs,
            my jaw,
my head.)
      (One day, brought (by car,
                no, by freight, by ferry)

           but could not rest.)
(One day, skipping electric & gas,

over the Hudson, the Missouri,
           the Mississippi
home, no
      free, no
        free
         & home.)

Crow's Head with Red Dahlias

Outside the peeling, gray barn, outside
the white house—low roof and green
shutters—where we will never live,
a crow dug its beak into the mud,
swallowed roots and tubers whole.
When we walked by again, black feathers
were wind-scattered into the fence. Scarlet
dahlias grew through sockets of crow skull.
Behind those chain links: white house
and gray barn—we will never know
their interiors, or perhaps only for one night
paling into morning, but for that passing
moment, next to you (Red, Red, Red,
Red) I was alive and happy.

Notes on the Poems

The epigraph for the collection originally appears in *The Poetry of Rilke*, translated by Edward Snow (North Point Press, 2009).

"Violets for Your Furs": the title is drawn from the title of a Dennis and Adair song, written in 1941.

"*the smoke of the country went up* ": the title is drawn from Genesis 19:28 (KJV).

"*whatever wilderness contained there* ": the quotation that forms the title appears in Cormac McCarthy's novel Blood Meridian (Random House, 1985).

"Arrival: Troy, New York": the epigraph for the poem originally appears as caption to the final panel in Jacob Lawrence's *The Migration Series* (1941).

"Liver of Sulfur": The line "the knife, so intimate, opening my throat" appears in Juan Luis Borges's "Conjectural Poem," translated by Alastair Reid and found in *The FSG Book of Twentieth-Century Latin American Poetry* (FSG, 2011).

"*dem kill my mama* ": the title is a lyric from Fela Kuti's song "Coffin for Head of State" (1981).

"On the Migration of Black Oystermen from Snow Hill, Maryland to Sandy Ground, Staten Island": the epigraph for the poem originally appears in Langston Hughes's poem "August 19th . . ." found in *The Collected Poems of Langston Hughes* (Vintage, 1995).

"*Love, oh love, oh careless love* ": the title is a lyric from the traditional song "Careless Love."

"*Where Do We Come From? What Are We? Where Are We Going?* ": the title is an English translation of the title to Paul Gauguin's painting *D'où Venons Nous / Que Sommes Nous / Où Allons Nous* (1898). The painting appeared in the Philadelphia Museum of Art's 2012 exhibition "Gauguin, Cézanne, Matisse: Visions of Arcadia."

"Tamir Rice": the epigraph for the poem originally appears in Emily Dickinson's poem "Sweet is the swamp with its secrets," found in *The Complete Poems of Emily Dickinson* (Back Bay Books, 1961).

"*Not on the sea, not on the sea*": the title is taken from Lord Byron's poem "Stanzas Composed During a Thunderstorm."

"Day 5 (Sunday): *lay thou thy basis sure*": the quotation in the title is taken from Act IV, scene iii, line 33 of Shakespeare's *Macbeth* (Folger Shakespeare Library, 2003).

"Ghost / Place / Sound (*This one's for you, Rex*)": the quotation in the title comes from a story, perhaps apocryphal, about Louis Armstrong. While giving a Buckingham Palace concert for George V of England, an insouciant Armstrong made this declaration as he began either a song or a trumpet solo. In section VI. of the poem, the sentence "*I growled it, smeared it, flatted it, sharped it*" is adapted from comments made by Sidney Bechet and found in Ted Gioia's *The History of Jazz,* Second Edition (Oxford UP, 2011).

ACKNOWLEDGMENTS

I wrote the words herein, but my support in doing so was legion. Thank you to Rachel Eliza Griffiths for her sisterhood, her bigheartedness, her example, and her poems, and for shepherding this book to a good home. Thank you to Dilruba Ahmed and Emily Pulfer-Terino for their friendship as well as for their careful, frank, and indispensable suggestions on a draft of this collection. Thank you to David Eye, Sean Singer, and Darren Wood for their camaraderie and for helpful suggestions on some individual poems. Thank you to the folks at Alice James Books, particularly Carey Salerno for believing in the book and for her expert suggestions, and Alyssa Neptune for guiding the book into its final form. Thank you to Patrick Corcoran, proprietor of Arcade Booksellers in Rye, NY, for keeping me well provisioned with reading material. Thank you to my friends from the following communities: New Hartford, Haverford College, the MFA Program at Syracuse University, Cave Canem (I remain forever a brick in the house), Philadelphia, Brewerytown/Fairmount, Springside Chestnut Hill Academy, the Solstice MFA Program, Ossining, and Rye Country Day School. You continue to sustain me with your kindness, intelligence, humanity, and beauty. Thank you to the Feinberg-Sage-Priest family, especially Alison, Barry, and Asher Feinberg for their generosity of love and their warm, welcoming embrace. Thank you to the Haley-Pollock-Simpson family, especially Mom, Dad, and Caitlin—you taught me to love, and daily I try to carry that gift forward. Thank you most of all to Naomi, Asa, and Isaac for their abiding love and joyful laughter, for making every day worth living, and for what is to come.

In addition, I wish to thank the editors of the publications where the following poems originally appeared, sometimes in earlier drafts, sometimes under different title:

Academy of American Poets *Poem-a-Day*, "Brewerytown," "*the smoke of the country went up*"
African American Review, "An Abridged History of American Violence"
American Poetry Review, "Arrival: Troy, New York," "Aubade," "Boxwood," "Indian & Colored Burial Ground," "The Road Will Be My Last Idea"
The Baffler, "Love, oh love, oh careless love"
Blackbird, "The Changing Table," "Liver of Sulfur"

Black Poets Speak Out, "Blue Jay Restaurant (29th & Girard)"

The Collagist, "Autumn: Far Field, New Moon"

Connotation Press: An Online Artifact, "An Old Country," "Grasping at Swallow's Tail," "The fig that, as it falls,"

Crab Orchard Review, "The Properties of Solid Phase Materials"

The Grief Diaries, "Dates & Inscriptions," "*dem kill my mama*"

Killens Review of Arts & Letters, "Fountain of the Three Rivers"

Poetry Northwest, "when mud daubers nest"

Poetrysociety.org, "Violets for Your Furs"

Public Pool, "On the Migration of Black Oystermen from Snow Hill, Maryland to Sandy Ground, Staten Island"

Smartish Pace, "Constellations of Our Own Making"

Solstice Literary Magazine, "Black Cock," "California Penal Code 484," "We, the Rubber Men"

The Spectacle, "Crow's Head with Red Dahlias," "GameStop," "Tamir Rice," "*whatever wilderness contained there,*"

Vinyl, "Day 5 (Sunday): *lay thou thy basis sure*"

In addition, I thank Thomas Dooley for including "Hurricane Season" in the February 2016 edition of his performance series Emotive Fruition.

BOOK BENEFACTORS

Alice James Books wishes to thank the following individuals who generously contributed toward the publication of *Ghost, like a Place*:

Shelley P. Haley & Adrian Pollock

For more information about AJB's book benefactor program, contact us via phone or email, or visit alicejamesbooks.org to see a list of forthcoming titles.

RECENT TITLES FROM ALICE JAMES BOOKS

Isako Isako, Mia Ayumi Malhotra
Of Marriage, Nicole Cooley
The English Boat, Donald Revell
We, the Almighty Fires, Anna Rose Welch
DiVida, Monica A. Hand
pray me stay eager, Ellen Doré Watson
Some Say the Lark, Jennifer Chang
Calling a Wolf a Wolf, Kaveh Akbar
We're On: A June Jordan Reader, Edited by Christoph Keller and Jan Heller Levi
Daylily Called It a Dangerous Moment, Alessandra Lynch
Surgical Wing, Kristin Robertson
The Blessing of Dark Water, Elizabeth Lyons
Reaper, Jill McDonough
Madwoman, Shara McCallum
Contradictions in the Design, Matthew Olzmann
House of Water, Matthew Nienow
World of Made and Unmade, Jane Mead
Driving without a License, Janine Joseph
The Big Book of Exit Strategies, Jamaal May
play dead, francine j. harris
Thief in the Interior, Phillip B. Williams
Second Empire, Richie Hofmann
Drought-Adapted Vine, Donald Revell
Refuge/es, Michael Broek
O'Nights, Cecily Parks
Yearling, Lo Kwa Mei-en
Sand Opera, Philip Metres
Devil, Dear, Mary Ann McFadden
Eros Is More, Juan Antonio González Iglesias, Translated by Curtis Bauer
Mad Honey Symposium, Sally Wen Mao
Split, Cathy Linh Che
Money Money Money | Water Water Water, Jane Mead
Orphan, Jan Heller Levi
Hum, Jamaal May
Viral, Suzanne Parker
We Come Elemental, Tamiko Beyer
Obscenely Yours, Angelo Nikolopoulos
Mezzanines, Matthew Olzmann
Lit from Inside: 40 Years of Poetry from Alice James Books, Edited by Anne Marie Macari and Carey Salerno

Alice James Books has been publishing poetry since 1973. The press was founded in Boston, Massachusetts as a cooperative wherein authors performed the day-to-day undertakings of the press. This collaborative element remains viable even today, as authors who publish with the press are also invited to become members of the editorial board and participate in editorial decisions at the press. The editorial board selects manuscripts for publication via the press's annual, national competition, the Alice James Award. AJB remains committed to its founders' original mission to support women poets, while expanding upon the scope to include poets of all genders, backgrounds, and stages of their careers. In keeping with our efforts to foster equity and inclusivity in publishing and the literary arts, AJB seeks out poets whose writing possesses the range, depth, and ability to cultivate empathy in our world and to dynamically push against silence. The press was named for Alice James, sister to William and Henry, whose extraordinary gift for writing went unrecognized during her lifetime.

Designed by Anna Reich
annareichdesign.com

Printed by McNaughton & Gunn